*"It's not what you gather,
but what you scatter."*

~

LIVING A LIFE

LARGER

THAN YOURSELF!

SUBESH RAMJATTAN

GREEN WINE™
FAMILY BOOKS

Copyright 2012 © by Subesh Ramjattan
Living A Life Larger Than Yourself
ISBN 978-1-935434-62-7

Library of Congress Control Number: 2011941265
Ramjattan, Subesh 1951—

> Subject Codes and Description: 1: PHI015000: Philosophy: Mind
> & Body; 2: SEL021000: Self Help: Motivational & Inspirational; 3:
> REL012120: Religion: Christian Life – Social Issues.

Printed in Australia, Brazil, France, Germany, Italy, Spain, UK, and USA and
anywhere there is an Espresso Book Machine

Cover Design by Global Graphics

Published by
GreenWine Family Books
A division of
GlobalEdAdvancePRESS
www.gea-books.com

DEDICATED
TO MY FRIENDS
WHO HAVE BEEN
WOUNDED IN THE DAILY
BATTLES OF LIFE.

~

Contents

"There is a good reward for hard work especially when the bottom line is to assist the less fortunate."

~

I. Keys to a Life Larger than Yourself

KEY ONE:
Understanding the lessons learned from your past.
"Look beyond the challenges of broken lives to the potential for a better life."

KEY TWO:
Volunteering – just find something to do, and do it.
"God keeps good records. You don't have to make headlines to make a difference."

KEY THREE:
See life as a partnership.
"You cannot give what you do not have. God blesses you to bless others."

KEY FOUR:
Live a faith-based life.
"God is the God of another chance."
"God did not comfort you to be comfortable, but to comfort others."

KEY FIVE:
Write a clear vision using faith-based ABC's of life.
Affection for children and families demonstrated
Business operation on faith-based principles
Contacts to build a resource network for the vision

KEY SIX:
Remember your Legacy – what you do for yourself will die with you; *what you do for others will last.*
"Invest in people, property, and poverty: The increase in value is worth the effort and has a good return on the investment."

Quality of Life Bridge

ALPHA

OMEGA

CARE FOR
THE CHILDREN

CARE FOR
THE ELDERLY

BRIDGE OVER TROUBLED WATER

ADULTS

II. Quality of Life for All

The Quality of Life Bridge is a way to connect to various aspects of an individual's personal and professional relationships throughout the human lifespan. The bridge becomes a way to link individuals to others who can assist their self-image and self-concept as a passageway to a better and improved quality of living. It is a way to assist individuals and couples across troubled waters and disappointment to a brighter future through improved self-confidence and improved beneficial relationships. Quality of life is usually determined by the general wellbeing of individuals in the normal aspects of daily life. The following acrostic identifies some of the aspects of a quality of life bridge.

III. An Acrostic for Quality of Life Bridge

Q uality is determined by attitude and action
U ltimately quality increases the quantity of life
A ctivities to insure that daily life has value
L iving a useful life produces true happiness
I ntervention to adjust areas of discontent
T otal life assessment to assure positive living
Y ielding gracefully to aging and the future

O pportunity to grow and develop personally
F aithfulness in personal and social relationships

L earning and sharing with others
I ncreasing the worth of friends
F uture healthy and comfortable state
E valuate and encourage a sense of well-being

B uilds passageways to a better outlook on life
R enewing personal and social commitments
I mproved intentionality of personal action
D eveloping problem-solving and social skills
G rowing older with dignity and self-respect
E njoying the stages of life without regret

IV. The Alpha and Omega

Alpha and Omega are used of Christ to denote His everlasting existence and means the beginning and the end. The concept of Alpha and Omega frames my spiritual work and deals with the beginning of life, the children and the ending of life, the senior, or elderly among us. The ministry of the Anapausis Community, the childcare at the

Bridge of Hope, and the personal ministry of my wife and I, also deals with all ages of people. We are concerned about the quality of life for each individual regardless of age and are particularly concerned about the empowerment of couples to live a quality life. The concept of Alpha and Omega ought to be used to guide and evaluate the development of community projects and services. At the Alpha end of life's continuum are the children who must have daily care and a safe place to live and grow within a family environment. On the Omega end of the continuum are the elderly who have a right to live and enjoy their golden years in peace and safety. In between are the adult years where the quality of life also matters.

V. Path to a Life of Quality

It is my firm conviction that when individuals and families show proper concern for their children and parents, that the path to a life of quality is open before them. When individuals neglect themselves, their children (or other people's children), and their parents or the elderly parents of others, they are on a slippery slope the end of which is misery and disappointment. It is also a conviction that a bridge can be constructed to assist adults over the troubled spots of life and improve both personal and professional relationships. It is a quality of life bridge.

KEY ONE:

Understanding the lessons learned from your past.

"Look beyond the challenges of broken lives to the potential for a better life."

VI. Cradle to the Grave

My basic concern is a life of quality for everyone from the cradle to the grave. Debbie and I have invested time, energy, and resources for child-care for the disadvantaged and housing for the elderly, known as Olive's House, initiated by funds from Debbie's grandmother. Between the cradle and the grave, we are attempting to build a Quality of Life Bridge to assist various phases of business and family life. One NGO that meets at Anapausis is known as Family Life of Trinidad and Tobago. Their motto is "help for today; hope for tomorrow." They identify five stages of Family Life beyond the childcare age and develop programs and training to meet the needs of each phase.

The stages of the Family Life Cycle with programs and training are:

1. Independence
2. Marriage
3. Parenting
4. The Empty Nest
5. Retirement and Senior Years.

VII. A Daily Guide to Quality of Life

To live a life of quality, one must daily work at improving their self-image and environment by maintaining an active and planned schedule. An unanticipated event may either be disruptive or an unexpected blessing. You must decide the value of an event and whether or not to permit the event to

KEY TWO:

Volunteering – just find something to do, and do it.

*"God keeps good records.
You don't have to make headlines
to make a difference."*

alter your plans. The confused and chaotic world will occupy you with "busyness" and intrude on your plans.

You must be aware of the emptiness of a busy life that leaves no time for faith, family or friends. Always take charge of your life and surroundings and claim periods of "rest" to bring a respite and provide breathing space for a productive life. It is the "rest" in music that makes the melody. You must daily write the melody line of your life and include the "rest notes" that provide the beat and tempo for your life. This is the only way to care for your spiritual heart and insure quality in your daily living.

VIII. Caring for Your Heart

Although the physical heart is vital to life, the health of the spiritual heart is essential to the quality of life. This critical aspect of living is the psychological center of emotional well-being and consists of three elements: the mind, the will, and the emotions.

Feed positive thoughts into your **mind** by reading good material, listening to good music, and talking with positive friends.

The **will** is the human decision-making mechanism and is cultivated by making good decisions that positively affect yourself and others.

Your **emotions** must be controlled.

KEY THREE:

See life as a partnership.

*"You cannot give what you do not have.
God blesses you to bless others."*

"Can two walk together, except they be agreed?"
(Amos 3:3)

IX. Positive Thoughts and Good Decisions

Emotional health depends on positive thoughts and good decisions plus constructive action daily that reinforces optimistic and affirmative attitudes. This works best when you remember that an attitude is a predisposition to act. A positive mental attitude provides a tendency toward feeding the best angels of your nature and breeds an optimistic and constructive frame of mind that becomes the threshold of true happiness.

X. Happiness is More than the Word

Real and true happiness is more than the word "happiness" alone implies. As the word is used today it relies on the little word "hap" which means "good luck or by chance." This suggests fate or luck or good fortune and these are far from true happiness. Happenstance does not create a quality of life. Happiness is a state you create. Only purposeful behavior that is more than activities can bring the deep satisfaction to life that many call "happiness." But there is a more classical view of "happiness" used by the ancient Greeks that is included in the word *eudaimonia* which comes only by a life well lived based on truth and virtue. It is this classical view that identifies the quality of life required to produce a life of faith and values. These positive virtues may be enhanced or improved by both action and attitude. When real happiness comes it will be based on truth and virtue.

KEY FOUR:

Live a faith-based life.

"God is the God of another chance."

*"God did not comfort you to be comfortable,
but to comfort others."*

XI. Attitude and Action

It seems that attitude and action are closely related. One cannot change their attitude by just changing their mind or thinking good thoughts. There must be action. For example, only a few individuals wake up each morning and really feel like jumping out of bed and facing the cruel world. In fact most of us would rather remain in bed "a little longer" but that doesn't change our mind. We still want a few more minutes. However, by acting promptly and getting out of bed, showering, and dressing for the day, one no longer wants to take a nap, but is ready for the challenges of the day. Action changed the attitude; doing something altered the predisposition to act; therefore, the path to positive daily living is an early and prompt action. Facing the world with a smile and confidence is good evidence of a life of quality.

XII. Ten Remedies for the Blues

If you feel down or dragging during the day, try one or two of these suggestions:

1. **Sing or hum an inspirational song.** A few minutes with a favorite tune can drastically change your outlook. This is an easy fix for the blues.
2. **Take a short walk and stretch.** The gentle and steady motion of a short walk starts up the production of "feel-good beta brain waves."
3. **Correct your posture, hold your head high.** It appears that the brain takes cues from good posture and alters neutron-transmitters to adjust your feeling of confidence.

KEY FIVE:

Write a clear vision using faith-based ABC's of life.

Affection for children and families demonstrated.
Business operation on faith-based principles.
Contacts to build a resource network for the vision.

4. **Limit your exposure to background noise.**
   Traffic or ringing phones can dampen your
   mood. If nothing else works, try ear plugs twice
   a day for short periods to limit the noise.

5. **Clean up your desk, car, or a closet.** Clutter
   dampens one's spirit.

6. **Practice gratitude** by letting others know how
   they have contributed to your life.

7. **Try a silent prayer or a calm period** of
   meditation to seek assistance of Providence.

8. **Eat healthy foods** that agree with you.

9. **Get sufficient peaceful sleep.**

10. **Do a friend a favor** or do someone's chore.
    This unselfish act will release the brain's ability
    to produce a steady stream of mood-boosting
    chemicals.

XIII. Eat Healthy

Physical health depends on eating right. Food
should be seen as fuel for the journey and not
used for comfort. Eat smaller portions. Include
vegetables and fruits. Stop when you feel full.
Overeating is a major cause of feeling bad about
yourself. Eating healthy will give you more energy
and assist with weight. Eating the right food at the
right time in the right amount will improve blood
pressure and cholesterol. It will also help prevent
heart problems both physically and emotionally.
Eating right is also a family event. The whole family
must be involved in the proper diet and proportions
to assist those who need the discipline the most.
Don't be a glutton when your partner or friend is
trying to lose weight.

KEY SIX:

Remember your Legacy – what you do for yourself will die with you; *what you do for others will last.*

*"Invest in people, property, and poverty:
The increase in value is worth the effort and
has a good return on the investment."*

XIV. The Big Question

The big question: how do we do this?
Think of your plate in sections. One half is for
vegetables and the other half is for proteins and
carbo-hydrates. If a quantity problem persists,
try a smaller plate. The same amount of food
on a smaller plate will look bigger and be more
satisfying. If you are still hungry after one plate full,
the next meal try drinking a glass of water before
the meal. Eat slower and try a salad or soup before
the main meal. If you have a portion problem,
permit someone else to prepare your plate and ask
that they not put the serving dishes on the table.
When you see more food you want more. If you
need a second helping, eat more vegetables. Learn
about whole grains and avoid the salt shaker. It
would be of great assistance to healthy eating to
learn portion size of different foods and identify the
unhealthy foods that are constantly on the table
or at least on the "menu." A good way is permit
someone to take your plate away as soon as you
have cleared it. As long as the plate is there you will
be tempted to eat more. Remember healthy eaters
consider food as fuel and do not overeat. The next
meal is just a few hours away.

XV. Be Active

A healthy life requires one to be active. Just
move. Walk if you can. Exercise any and every way
you can. Work in the yard or the garden. Ride a
stationary bike. Dance if you have moves; if not,
just move. Swimming or water aerobics are good.

Apply the cleansing power of forgiveness directly
on the wounded area of your life.

Stay safe while you exercise. You should still be able to carry on a conversation with a friend or recite a poem or song to yourself. If breathing gets hard stop and take a 2 minute rest and begin again. Remember, walking is more relaxing when you have someone with whom to carry on a conversation. The time goes by faster and friendships are strengthened.

XVI. Understand Your Feelings

Each individual is a unique human being. There is no one else just the same; therefore, what others may say or think about you is of little consequence. You must know yourself and understand your feelings. Know when you need medication, when food or medicine is changing your attitude or the way you deal with others. Always speak to a medical professional about this difficulty (you do not need the advice of friends). Everyone gets upset and occasionally angry or irritable, but you must know when this behavior is being produced by the way you feel. Don't forget how many people care about you. Maintain a conversational connection with as many friends as possible and still maintain your normal life. However, don't let "friends" control your life and don't let the "telephone, cell, or the email" establish your schedule or the pace of the day. If you feel sad or down, do something: stay busy, do something productive, this will bring quality to your life.

"...consecrate and purify it with the cleansing water of the Word... "

(Ephesians 5:26 DNT)

XVII. Face the Future with Confidence

Fear of the future can destroy the quality of life. Everyone has difficulties. All grow older. Life itself is an up and down proposition. There are hills and valleys. Good times and bad times. Just don't let life get you down. If life serves you "lemons" make "lemonade" for yourself and others.

Tomorrow can be better than today provided you develop a positive attitude. Expect the best and leave the rest to God. In fact, worry is taking responsibility for things that belong to others. When "something" is beyond arms reach, leave it in God's hands. Providence knows best how to handle such things. Just live day by day expecting tomorrow to be better. This will bring quality into your daily life. This is living the good life that produces quality.

XVIII. The Concept of Quality

What is quality? Several words assist the understanding of the concept of quality, such as **advantage, control, excellence, importance, meaning, merit, power, status,** and **usefulness**. Let us look at each of these words and see how they expand the concept of quality.

Advantage – describes a plus, a benefit, an improvement.

Control – includes manage, organize, direct, influence.

Excellence – denotes quality, distinction, brilliance.

1. Sing or hum an inspirational song.

A few minutes with a favorite tune can drastically change your outlook. This is an easy fix for the blues.

Importance – indicates worth, value, significance, substance.

Merit – involves something deserved or earned.

Power – suggests energy, strength, vitality, enthusiasm.

Status – shows prominence, importance, position, standing.

Usefulness – designates effectiveness, convenience, helpfulness.

XIX. Qualify of Life Concerns

Listed below are a dozen areas of primary concern when considering the quality of life for adults:

- **Attitude Toward Social Change**
- **Feelings About the Underprivileged**
- **Emotional Life**
- **Faith-based Connections**
- **Financial Affairs**
- **Health and Fitness**
- **Love Relationship**
- **Parenting Skills**
- **Personal Nourishment**
- **Social Relationships**
- **Spiritual Development**
- **Work or Professional Life**

2. Take a short walk and stretch.

The gentle and steady motion of a short walk starts up the production of "feel-good beta brain waves."

XX. A Rationale for Dealing with Individuals

A rationale for dealing with the "Quality of Life"relates directly to the Alpha and Omega, the beginning and the end. In the work between children and the elderly, the Quality of Life effort is to build a bridge across the adult years until retirement. These are the most productive and problematic years of life for most people. Scripture declared, "Man that is born of woman is of few years and full of trouble." Most of the medical and religious efforts deal with these troubles. When one is dealing with adults with difficulties or weakened quality of life, it is usually because of poor self-image, a bad marriage, financial difficulties, or perhaps a wealthy person useing money as a pacifier in an attempt to buy happiness.   The truly happy people are those who serve others and put themselves in the background.

XXI. Evaluate the General Well-being

The term "quality of life" is used to identify the general well-being of individuals. The term is used widely in different contexts: in this case, it deals only with an intervention in the lives of individuals with general dissatisfaction with their personal or professional life. Quality of life should not be confused with the concept of standard of living, which is based primarily on income. While Quality of Life has long been both an explicit or implicit goal for my work, an adequate definition and measurement have been elusive. There are both objective and subjective indicators across a range

3.   Correct your posture, hold your head high.

It appears that the brain takes cues from good posture and alters neutron-transmitters to adjust your feeling of confidence.

of disciplines and scales, and recent work on the subjective well-being surveys and the psychology and philosophy of happiness have spurred renewed interest.

Included in related concepts to quality is the use of faith-based principles to guide both life and living. When life is related to faith in a Higher Power as a Guide, a better quality of life is the normal outcome. General happiness is a byproduct of this quality of life.

XXII. A Quality of Life Survey

A Quality of Life Survey Instrument could be used as a screening tool for individuals who desire significant change in various areas of their life. Results would highlight areas that may require change to improve their quality of life. The survey instrument could gather data on the relationship between an individual's quality of life and other behaviors. This would be an assessment using indirect measurements to develop a basis for guidance and mentoring individuals and couples. Major areas for consideration in a survey would be:

- **Aesthetic Satisfaction**
- **Benevolent Behavior**
- **Career/Work Satisfaction**
- **Communications Behavior**
- **Emotional Maturity**
- **Extended Family Relations**
- **Faith-based Concerns**

4. Limit your exposure to background noise.

Traffic or ringing phones can dampen your mood. If nothing else works, try ear plugs twice a day for short periods to limit the noise.

- **Financial Security**
- **Future Concerns**
- **Happiness Measure**
- **Health/Fitness Measure**
- **Inter-personal Relations**
- **Leisure/Vacation Behavior**
- **Marital Relations**
- **Parenting Relations**
- **Personal Growth**
- **Physical Fitness Indicators**
- **Security Concerns**
- **Self-Image Concerns**
- **Social Activity**
- **Daily Stress Level**
- **Sense of Well-Being**

To participate in a Quality of Life Survey contact
subesh60@gmail.com

XXIII. Concepts Related to Quality

Also related are concepts such as personal freedom, individual rights, and happiness that have intruded on marriage and family as well as the professional and business areas. Since so many of the indicators are subjective and cannot be directly measured; it becomes necessary to develop an instrument to surrogate these qualities and assess them indirectly. For example, "How much does a man love his wife?" This cannot be directly

5. Clean up your desk, car, or a closet.

Clutter dampens one's spirit.

measured but must be indirectly assessed through a developed index. What is obvious is that increased income or actual wealth does not directly impact the Quality of Life. Consequently, standard of living should not be taken as criteria for quality of life. Yet, several assessed areas may be considered as having some influence on the quality of life.

It is a clear conviction that faith-based principles and the qualities of spiritual development can greatly influence the quality of life for adults. Adequate spiritual development can assist an individual or a couple over the troubled waters of life and bring a renewed quality and quantity to relationships. A survey instrument could be used to assess the areas of weakness that impact quality of life for individuals in their marriage, interpersonal relationships, career and professional life.

XXIV. The Pursuit of Happiness

No community effort, program or service is complete that does not take into consideration the needs of children, the elderly and all the adult dynamics that are a part of the process from birth to death. The primary concern is for the children because they represent the future. At the other end of the journey are the elderly with their needs and wants. In between the children and the elderly are the lives of many adults who live without the quality of life needed to assure that life is worth living. Some call this happiness, while others see contentment and pleasure coming from the use of faith-based principles and the addition of spiritual

6. **Practice gratitude** by letting others know how they have contributed to your life.

worship. In reality life is a journey, and the adult pursuit of happiness normally needs a little guidance to focus on the objective and proper goals in life and career. It is the pursuit of happiness. Life is not always a bed of roses or all circumstances are not pleasant and all the people with whom we come in contact are not always filled with gladness. However, I believe there is a place, built on faith-based principles, that becomes the foundation for a life of quality and peace.

XXV. Pure Religion Before God

Holy Scripture is clear that pure religion is to look after the women alone and the fatherless in order to keep them from being tainted with negative feelings. To overlook these circumstances is to bring greater condemnation upon all who neglect the needs of orphans (the fatherless) and women who are struggling alone to care for their children.

XXVI. Transparency in Belief and Conduct

Free from all that would dim the transparency in belief and conduct before God and the Father is this, to go see and relieve the orphans without a father's protection and the women lacking a husband in their distress, and to keep himself untainted with guilt. (James 1:27 DNT)

7. Try a silent prayer or a calm period
of meditation to seek assistance of
Providence.

~

Develop a relationship with God.

XXVII. The Wound Wash Process

"...consecrate and purify it with the
cleansing water of the Word..."
(Ephesians 5:26 DNT)

Everyone has wounds. Most wounds, hurts, or offenses come from a loved one or a close friend. Those whom you love can hurt you the most, even a friend can offend; however, simple "forgiveness" is the secret to purifying the wound and starting the healing process.

Follow these seven steps:

1. **Before starting** the WOUND WASH process, pray a simple prayer to clear your mind.

2. **Then, forgive** the one who caused the wound.

3. **Now, read** Ephesians 5:15-33 (DNT)

15. Look carefully how you walk, not foolishly, but in the light,   16. buying up every opportunity, because these are evil days.   17. Wherefore be not reckless, but prudently understand the will of the Lord.   18. Stop excessively drinking wine, which produces riotous living; more willingly be soaked with the Spirit;   19. but speak to one another in exalted verse, songs of praise, and sacred music, singing and making melody with the music of your hearts, to the Lord;   20. continue giving thanks to God the Father for all things in the name of our Lord Jesus Christ;   21. line up under one another in reverence to Christ.   22. Wives, line up under and adapt to your own husbands, as unto the Lord.   23. For the husband is in charge of the wife,

☺

Stop complaining - start living!

even as Christ is in charge of the church: and he is the champion of the church.   24. Therefore as the church is to line up under the authority of Christ, so let the wives line up under their husbands in all things.   25. Husbands, be devoted to your wives, even as Christ is devoted to the church, and gave himself for it;   26. that he might consecrate and purify it with the cleansing water of the Word,   27. that he might present the church to himself as a glorious bride, without spot, wrinkle or blemish.   28. So must men love their wives as if they were their own body. He who loves his wife loves himself.   29. For no man ever loathed his own body; but nourishes and values it, even as the Lord values the church: 30. for we are members of his body.   31. For this reason shall a man leave his father and mother and cleave intimately to his wife, and they shall become one new body.   32. This is a great sacred secret: but I speak concerning Christ and the church.   33. Nevertheless let each one in particular love his wife even as himself; and the wife should respect her husband.

4. Apply the cleansing power of forgiveness directly on the wounded area of your life.

5. Flush the wounded area freely with fresh prayer and thanksgiving for the better things in life.

6. Now, read 1 Peter 4:7-11 (DNT)

7. The end of all things is near: live wisely, and keep your senses awake to greet the times of prayer.   8. Above all embrace each other in love that is constant and intense: because love covers a multitude of sins. 9. Never grudge the hospitality you show one another. 10. As each has received a gift from God, so let all use such gifts in the service of one another, as good stewards of God's multi-sided grace.   11. Should any man speak, let him speak words sent from God; if a man serves, let him do it with God-given ability: that God may be glorified in all things through Jesus Christ, to whom be praise and dominion forever and ever. Amen.

7. The WOUND WASH Process may be applied as often as needed.

~

AMEN

— so be it —

~

**Additional copies of this book and others
by Subesh Ramjattan can be secured from:**

www.gea-books.com or

From the Author: subesh60@gmail.com or

Amazon, Barnes&Nobel and other web sites or

Anyplace there is an Espresso Book Machine

Printed in Australia, Brazil, France, Germany, Italy, Spain, UK, and USA

www.ingramcontent.com/pod-product-compliance
Lightning Source LLC
Chambersburg PA
CBHW030308030426
42337CB00012B/632